*O*prah

WINFREY

Biography®

Oprah WINFREY

Katherine Krohn

*Lerner Publications Company*
*Minneapolis*

*This book is dedicated to my dad, Don Ray Krohn*

*This book is available in two editions:*
Library binding by Lerner Publications Company,
 a division of Lerner Publishing Group
Soft cover by First Avenue Editions,
 an imprint of Lerner Publishing Group
241 First Avenue North
Minneapolis, MN 55401 U.S.A.

Website address: www.lernerbooks.com

Library of Congress Cataloging-in-Publication Data

Krohn, Katherine E.
 Oprah Winfrey / by Katherine Krohn.
  p.  cm. — (A&E biography)
 Includes bibliographical references and index.
 ISBN: 0-8225-4999-9 (lib. bdg. : alk. paper)
 ISBN: 0-8225-5000-8 (pbk. : alk. paper)
  1. Winfrey, Oprah—Juvenile literature.  2. Television personalities—United States—Biography—Juvenile literature.  3. Motion picture actors and actresses—United States—Biography—Juvenile literature.
 [1. Winfrey, Oprah.  2. Television personalities.  3. Actors and Actresses.  4. African Americans—Biography.  5. Women—Biography.]  I. Title.  II. Biography (Lerner Publications Company)
 PN1992.4.W56 K76  2002
 791.45'028'092—dc21                                    00-013122

Manufactured in the United States of America
1  2  3  4  5  6  –  JR  –  07  06  05  04  03  02

# CONTENTS

Oprah spent her early childhood on a farm in rural Mississippi, similar to the one shown above.

# *Chapter* **ONE**

# FARM GIRL

**F**OUR-YEAR-OLD OPRAH WINFREY STOOD ON THE
screened-in back porch on her grandmother's small
farm in rural Mississippi. Oprah watched her grandmother, Hattie Mae Lee, stir and poke at a big black
iron pot of boiling clothes. It was 1958, and Hattie Mae
couldn't afford an electric washing machine. Instead,
she cleaned her family's dirty clothes in boiling water.

"I remember thinking, my life won't be like this . . . it
will be better," Oprah said later. "And it wasn't from a
place of arrogance, it was just a place of knowing that
things could be different for me somehow."

Oprah Gail Winfrey was born in her grandmother's
house in Kosciusko, a small town in central Mississippi, on January 29, 1954. She was born with the

help of a midwife, a woman who delivers babies. Oprah's mother, Vernita Lee, was eighteen, unmarried, and not in a serious relationship with the baby's father. He was Vernon Winfrey, a twenty-five-year-old U.S. Army private stationed at Fort Rucker, Alabama. The new unnamed baby girl was the great-great-granddaughter of Constantine and Violet Winfrey, a Mississippi slave couple who had been freed after the Civil War.

Vernita wasn't sure what to name the new baby at first. A week after the birth, Vernita's sister, Ida, suggested that Vernita name the new member of the family after a character in the Bible—Orpah, in the Book of Ruth. But the name was misspelled on the baby's birth certificate as "Oprah," and that's how it has been spoken and written ever since.

During the 1950s, many African Americans in the small towns of the South were still hurting financially from the Great Depression. This economic crisis had crippled the United States in the 1930s and early 1940s and left many people without jobs and homes. Many black southerners, tired of being poor, moved to northern states in search of work. Cities like Detroit, Cleveland, Milwaukee, and New York offered better opportunities for employment.

Oprah was only four years old when her mother decided to pack her bags and move to Milwaukee, Wisconsin—without Oprah. In Milwaukee Vernita hoped to find work as a maid and make a better life for herself. She planned to send for her daughter once she found work in the city.

Oprah turned to her grandmother, whom she called Mama, for love and guidance. Mama was very strict, but she also cared deeply for Oprah.

## CHORES AND CHURCH

Hattie Mae lived on the outskirts of town, and there were no other children nearby. Oprah yearned for playmates. Instead of befriending children, she made friends with the animals on the farm, giving names to the chickens and pigs and telling them stories.

From an early age, Oprah was expected to do chores around the farm. Her grandmother taught her to hang the freshly hand-washed laundry on the clothesline with wooden clothespins. She also showed Oprah how to make soap from lye, a strong-smelling, powdery white chemical.

"Watch me, 'cause you're going to have to learn how to do this," said Hattie Mae. But Oprah had different plans for her future. "Don't need to watch Grandma," she thought, "because my life isn't going to be like this."

Hattie Mae's house did not have indoor plumbing. Oprah's main chore was to haul water from the well, located several yards from the house, every morning and night. Oprah and her grandmother used the water for drinking, washing dishes, and cleaning themselves with a washcloth. On Saturday nights, Oprah received her weekly tub bath, using water heated on the stove. The next day, she and Mama would be fresh and clean for church.

Oprah's family couldn't afford store-bought toys. She had a favorite doll that her grandmother made from a corncob. Although the doll was plain, Oprah thought she was beautiful.

Hattie Mae wanted Oprah to grow up reading the Bible, so she taught her to read when she was only three years old. She encouraged her to memorize passages from the Bible and other religious books. Young Oprah had a phenomenal memory. She quickly memorized her Bible verses. Hattie Mae was proud of her granddaughter and wanted to show her off. Hattie Mae arranged for Oprah to speak at church services on Easter Sunday.

"Little Mistress Winfrey will render a recitation," announced the preacher at Kosciusko Baptist Church. Oprah stood up for her very first public speaking appearance. She smiled and spoke confidently in her high-pitched, little-girl voice.

"Jesus rose on Easter Day, Hallelujah, Hallelujah . . . all the angels did proclaim," she recited.

Hattie Mae smiled proudly from the front-row pew. A woman sitting nearby leaned toward her. "[Hattie Mae], this child is gifted," she whispered, fanning herself with a paper fan.

Oprah's grandmother nodded as the church people praised Oprah's speaking ability. The whole congregation was awestruck that a small child could speak so eloquently.

Oprah had other occasions to recite when Hattie Mae had company over to the house. "I would just get up in front of her friends and start doing pieces I had memorized," Oprah said. "Everywhere I went, I'd say, 'Do you want to hear me do something?'"

While Oprah was encouraged to recite Bible passages, at most other times she was discouraged from talking in public. Hattie Mae, like many people in her generation, expected children to be "seen and not heard." Children were supposed to remain quiet except when spoken to by an adult.

Oprah's grandmother also believed in the Bible phrase, "Spare the rod and spoil the child." In other words, she felt that children who did not receive physical punishment would grow up to be spoiled and disrespectful. Oprah, lively and full of spirit, was strictly disciplined.

Oprah's heart sank whenever her grandmother told her to "go get a switch." That meant Oprah had done something that displeased her grandmother and that Oprah was in for another "switching," or beating with a stick. She had to cut a tree branch herself and bring it to her grandmother.

Oprah figured that white children never got beatings. She thought they must have perfect lives. Oprah admired the happy, glamorous film stars she saw when she went to the movie theater with her grandmother. She especially liked Shirley Temple, a cheerful child movie star with shiny blond curls and an upturned nose. Oprah wanted to be just like Shirley Temple.

"I used to sleep with a clothespin on my nose, and two cotton balls," Oprah recalled. "And I couldn't breathe. And all I would do is wake up with two clothespin prints on the side of my nose, trying to get it to turn up."

## SCHOOL DAYS

In the fall of 1959, Oprah entered kindergarten in the nearby town of Buffalo, Mississippi. Unlike the other children in her class, five-year-old Oprah could already read and write, and she quickly became bored with the simple play and basic lessons of kindergarten.

One day soon after school began, Oprah wrote a note to her teacher, Miss Knew. She handed the teacher the note. The teacher read the carefully printed words: "DEAR MISS NEW [sic]. I DO NOT THINK I BELONG HERE."

The teacher was astonished that Oprah could already write. Without hesitation, she arranged for Oprah to be moved into the first-grade class.

Soon Oprah faced a different kind of move. Within the year, her grandmother became ill, and Oprah was sent to live with her mother in Milwaukee. Oprah left Mississippi, and her grandmother, forever.

## RACE RELATIONS IN THE 1950s

hen Oprah was a child, racial prejudice was common in the United States, especially in the southern states. For decades, many public schools in the United States were segregated—black kids went to all-black schools and white kids went to all-white schools. In 1954, the year Oprah was born, the U.S. Supreme Court made a decision that ended racial segregation in public schools.

However, other public places in the South remained segregated. Black citizens were banned from using "whites only" drinking fountains, rest rooms, and other facilities. Racially segregated hotels, churches, train and bus stations, theaters, and restaurants were common. On buses, black passengers were required to sit in a separate section at the back of the bus. They had to give up their seat if a white person wanted to sit there.

In December 1955, a forty-two-year-old African American seamstress, Rosa Parks, refused to give up her seat on a bus in Montgomery, Alabama, to a white man who wanted to sit in her row. Parks was arrested. Her courageous action inspired other African Americans to protest her arrest and the bus segregation laws. Martin Luther King Jr., a Baptist minister, and other activists organized a 382-day boycott of Montgomery's bus system by black riders.

In his first speech to the protesters, King said, "We have no alternative but to protest. For many years we have shown an amazing patience. . . . But we come here tonight to be saved from that patience that makes us patient with anything less than freedom and justice."

In 1956, thanks to the efforts of Rosa Parks, King, and the thousands of black citizens who refused to ride the Montgomery buses, the bus company desegregated its facilities, and protesters began picketing and boycotting segregated facilities in other communities. The Civil Rights movement was well under way.

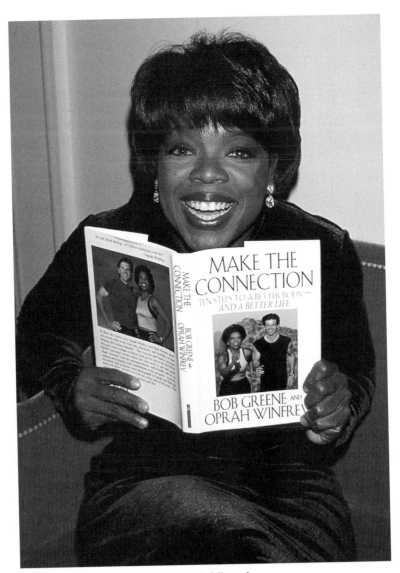

*Oprah has loved books since childhood.*

*Chapter* **TWO**

# WHERE IS HOME?

**O**PRAH'S MOTHER GRABBED OPRAH'S BOOK OUT OF her hand. Six-year-old Oprah felt her pulse race and her face get hot.

"You're nothing but a bookworm!" her mother yelled. "You think you're better than other kids! Get your butt outside!"

Oprah fought back tears and reluctantly went outside. What was wrong with loving books? she wondered.

Vernita Lee, Oprah's mother, was raised with little education, and she didn't understand the beauty and power of books. Not only did she discourage her daughter from reading, but she refused to take Oprah to the public library, the place she most wanted to go.

Oprah didn't like her new home in Milwaukee, an

industrial city that was noisy and crowded with people. Everything seemed so strange and different from
life on the farm in Kosciusko. Oprah missed her
grandmother, her teacher and schoolmates, and people at church.

Vernita lived in a single room in a boardinghouse
on Ninth Street. She worked as a maid, cleaning the
homes of white people. Unfortunately, her wages were
lower than she had hoped to earn. And Vernita had
two children to feed. She had recently given birth to
her second child, Patricia. Oprah now had a baby
half sister.

Even though Vernita worked long, difficult hours, she
sometimes had to rely on welfare (funds provided by
the U.S. government to low-income families) to make
ends meet. She had little time to care for Oprah and
the new baby. When Vernita did have time at home,
she showered the baby with affection, ignoring Oprah.

"[Patricia] was adored because she was light-
skinned," Oprah said later. "My half sister and mother
slept inside. I was put out on the porch."

## UPROOTED AGAIN

Oprah's mother felt overwhelmed with the demands of
working at her job and raising two children. She often
left Oprah and Patricia with neighbors in the boardinghouse or with a cousin who lived nearby. A little
over a year after Oprah moved in with her mother,
Vernita decided that Oprah should go stay with her

father in Nashville, Tennessee, for a while. In the meantime, Vernita figured, she would look for a better home for her daughters.

Oprah didn't know her father, Vernon Winfrey, very well. She hadn't seen him since she was a small child. And she had never been to Tennessee. She wasn't sure what to expect.

In the mid-1950s, after his service in the U.S. Army, Vernon had moved to Nashville, a big, prosperous city known as the home of the country music industry. Vernon had married a woman named Zelma and bought a one-story brick house with white shutters. He worked two jobs as a janitor, at a hospital and at Vanderbilt University in Nashville.

Vernon and Zelma were delighted to have seven-year-old Oprah join their household. They loved kids and were unable to have children of their own. Oprah felt welcome in their home immediately. She was thrilled to discover that, for the first time in her life, she would have her own bedroom and bed.

Because Oprah was ahead of most children her age, she was advanced a grade in her new school, Wharton Elementary School, in Nashville. Her father and stepmother wanted Oprah to be prepared for third grade, so they spent many hours with her, helping her learn her multiplication tables and strengthen her spelling and vocabulary skills.

Vernon and Zelma were strict parents. They believed that children needed structure in their lives. And, although Vernon and Zelma were not educated themselves, they understood the importance of schoolwork and reading.

## A READER AND SPEAKER

Oprah's father and stepmother took her to the library soon after she arrived in Nashville. To Oprah's delight, they insisted that she get a library card. "Getting my library card was like citizenship, it was like American citizenship," remembered Oprah.

Oprah liked to daydream, and sometimes she imagined herself as a character in the book she was reading. "I read a book in the third grade about Katie John, who hated boys, and she had freckles," said Oprah. "Well, Lord knows, I'm not going to have freckles, no way, no how. But I tried to put some on. And I went through 'my Katie John phase.'"

Vernon and Zelma required Oprah to write book reports on the books she checked out of the library, in addition to completing her regular school assignments. Oprah didn't mind the extra work. She liked to read and study, and she liked the fact that her father and stepmother paid so much attention to her.

Vernon and Zelma were active members of Faith Missionary Baptist Church in Nashville. They were pleased to see how well Oprah could recite Bible passages and stories. Oprah began speaking in church, as she had in Kosciusko.

On one occasion, she recited a sermon called

James Weldon Johnson was an inspiring writer as well as a civil rights activist.

"Invictus" by William Ernest Henley. "At the time I was saying it, I didn't know what I was talking about," Oprah recalled, "but I'd do all the motions, 'O-U-T OF THE NIGHT THAT covers me,' and people would say, 'Whew, that child can speak.'"

Oprah especially liked the sermons of James Weldon Johnson, an author who lived from 1871 to 1938. Johnson had been a newspaper editor, a lawyer, and field secretary for the National Association for the Advancement of Colored People, the nation's first civil rights organization. Johnson's sermons and poems were based on the books of the Bible. Oprah read one of his poems, "The Creation," in church: "And God stepped out on space,/And he looked around and said:/I'm lonely—I'll make me a world. . . ."

Vernon and Zelma took Oprah to speak at churches all over Nashville. She became known as "the Speaker"—the young girl who could speak so well. With her talents encouraged and blossoming in Nashville, Oprah felt truly happy for the first time in a long time.

*Oprah moved back to Milwaukee,* above, *in 1962.*

*Chapter* **THREE**

# THE PREACHER

**W**HEN THE SCHOOL YEAR ENDED IN **1962,** EIGHT-year-old Oprah traveled back to Milwaukee for a summer visit with her mother. When Oprah saw her mother again, she was surprised. So much had changed in the past year.

Vernita had moved with Patricia to a two-bedroom apartment. Oprah's mother also had another baby, a boy named Jeffrey. In Milwaukee, Oprah shared a bedroom with her half brother and half sister. She spent the summer reading and looking after her younger siblings, Patricia and Jeffrey. She didn't see much of her mother, who worked long hours. When Vernita was home, she spent most of her time caring for her youngest children.

As autumn approached, Vernon arrived in Milwaukee to take Oprah back to Nashville. But Oprah told him she wanted to stay in Milwaukee. She missed her father, her stepmother, and her house in Nashville, but she wanted to please her mother. Disappointed, Vernon returned by himself to Nashville.

Oprah busied herself with schoolwork. She liked the fourth grade. She especially admired her teacher, Mrs. Mary Duncan. Mrs. Duncan treated Oprah like she was a special person. She gave Oprah attention and guidance, which she wasn't getting from her mother.

When Oprah was young, many public schools set aside time during the day for "devotion"—Bible readings, religious lessons, and prayer. Because Oprah was such a good speaker, Mrs. Duncan often asked her to lead the daily devotion in class. Some of Oprah's classmates didn't like her, because she was smart and good at reciting. They nicknamed her "Preacher Woman."

Each Sunday in church, Oprah would memorize the minister's sermon. Then, during the devotion periods at school the next week, while her classmates snacked on graham crackers and milk, Oprah recited bits and pieces of the sermon.

"My, my, that's just lovely, Miss Oprah Gail," Mrs. Duncan said.

## LONELY GIRL

At home, Oprah didn't get nearly as much attention. She often turned to television for company. TV was a relatively new phenomenon in the early 1960s. Back in 1951, the very first "coast-to-coast" television programming was broadcast in the United States. But most U.S. households did not own a television set until the late 1950s or early 1960s.

Oprah's favorite TV shows were about happy families. She loved *Leave It to Beaver*, a funny sitcom about a boy named Beaver Cleaver and his family. She also enjoyed the popular show *I Love Lucy*, featuring the madcap adventures of comedian Lucille Ball. Oprah thought she might want to be an actress someday, a famous star like the ones she saw on television and in movies.

Oprah continued to recite sermons and stories in church. She loved to speak—for anyone who would listen. "From the time I was eight years old, I was a champion speaker," she said. "I spoke for every women's group, banquet, church function—I did the circuit."

Oprah loved the attention and praise she received when she spoke in public. But privately, she was a lonely child who craved love and affection from her mother. Unfortunately, Vernita was usually too busy to give Oprah the care and attention she wanted.

Vernita often left Oprah and her half brother and half sister with a babysitter. One evening when Oprah was nine years old, her mother went out and left the children in the care of their nineteen-year-old cousin. That night, Oprah's cousin raped her. Afterward, she was trembling and shaking and crying. Her cousin took her out for an ice cream cone and told her not to tell anyone what he had done.

A couple of years after the assault, Oprah was sexually abused by a family friend and then by an uncle. For several years, Oprah endured repeated sexual abuse. "It was just an ongoing, continuous thing," she later said. "So much so, that I started to think, you know, 'This is the way life is.'"

At the time, Oprah blamed herself for the ongoing abuse. She carried "a big, looming dark secret in [her] heart" and lived in constant fear and worry. "Every time I had a stomachache, I thought I was pregnant," she said.

When Oprah was a child, there was little public awareness of childhood sexual abuse. It was not discussed openly, and no laws existed to protect children. Oprah figured that no one would believe her if she told the truth or that she would be blamed for being sexually abused. So, feeling confused and helpless, she kept silent. She tried not to think about the abuse. She concentrated on doing her schoolwork, reciting in church, and reading.

In books, Oprah could lose herself in other worlds and forget her troubles for a while. When she was a young teenager, Oprah's favorite book was Betty Smith's *A Tree Grows in Brooklyn*, the story of Francie Nolan, a lonely but hopeful poor girl growing up in Brooklyn, New York, in the early 1900s.

Oprah stayed up all night long reading the book in the small bedroom that she shared with Patricia and Jeffrey. "There was a tree outside my apartment, and I used to imagine it was the same tree," remembered Oprah. "I felt like my life was like [Francie Nolan's]."

Despite her difficulties at home, Oprah did well in school and earned good grades. But she withdrew from people and had few friends.

## UPWARD BOUND

In the seventh grade, Oprah started attending Lincoln Middle School in downtown Milwaukee. Gene Abrams, one of the teachers at Lincoln, observed Oprah reading in the school cafeteria every day. Oprah stood out from the other students. She wasn't rowdy and loud. She wasn't surrounded by chatty friends like the other girls. Instead, she was quiet and studious, always reading a book.

Abrams arranged for her to be transferred to Nicolet High School, an all-white school in the Milwaukee suburb of Glendale. There, Oprah could take part in a program called Upward Bound, an effort to give underprivileged but academically advanced students a better education.

Oprah was both excited and nervous about changing schools. Her daily routine changed dramatically. She had to ride three buses to get to the suburban school, and she was the only African American student there. Oprah spoke with a southern accent, so she didn't talk

*Oprah was the only African American sophomore at Nicolet High School in 1969.*

like the other kids, either. Most of the students at Nicolet were nice to Oprah, and she quickly made friends. But she wasn't sure if people liked her because of who she was or because she was black. "In 1968 it was real hip to know a black person, so I was very popular," Oprah recalled.

When Oprah returned home each day, she could see too clearly the contrast between her life and the lives of her privileged white friends. She felt poor. She wished she had nice clothes and a big house like the kids at Nicolet High.

Although she liked her friends, she couldn't relate to them. The students at Nicolet had had very little exposure to black people—and it showed. "The kids would all bring me back to their houses, pull out their Pearl Bailey albums, bring out their maid from the back and say, 'Oprah, do you know Mabel?'" Oprah remembered.

One of Oprah's friends, Rita, asked her if she knew Sammy Davis Jr., a popular black singer. "They figured all blacks knew each other. It was real strange and real tough," said Oprah.

## TROUBLED TEEN

Life at home was also difficult. Oprah still yearned for more affection from her mother, who seemed to favor Patricia and Jeffrey. Meanwhile, she suffered ongoing sexual abuse. She had no one to talk to about her experience and feelings, and that only made things worse. Her unhappiness began to be reflected in her behavior, as she "acted out" and became wilder during her teen years.

In 1968, when Oprah was fourteen, she was having trouble reading. Her mother took her to an eye doctor, who told Oprah that she needed bifocal glasses. In the late 1960s, bifocals had two separate lenses, which were visible in the glass. The lenses were bad enough, but Oprah's mother also chose the least expensive frames for the eyeglasses, a pair of old-fashioned "butterfly" rims.

"I felt so bad about wearing these glasses that I said to my mother one day, I said, 'Mom, I think [we] need to talk about this because I'm really an ugly child,'" Oprah recalled.

Oprah wanted a pair of stylish, attractive glasses, but Vernita told her they couldn't afford nicer frames. But Oprah wasn't ready to give up.

She waited until her mother left for work one day. Then Oprah stomped on the new glasses, crushing them to bits. To make the living room look like the scene of a crime, she knocked a lamp to the floor and tore down the curtains. Next she called the police. "We've been robbed," she cried. "Robbed!"

When the police arrived at the apartment, Oprah was sprawled on the floor. She pretended to be unconscious, as if someone had hit her on the head and knocked her out. The officer was suspicious. He thought Oprah might be faking the robbery.

But when Oprah "came to," the officer took her to the hospital. Workers there called Oprah's mother, who rushed to the hospital in a panic. Vernita, too, wondered if Oprah was acting, but she wasn't sure. In the end, Oprah's elaborate scheme worked. Her mother bought her a new pair of glasses.

Oprah's behavior grew more and more dramatic. She skipped school, dated many boys, stole money from her mother's purse, and ran away from home more than once.

One time when Oprah ran away, she headed for downtown Milwaukee, where she saw a big limousine stopped in front of a fancy hotel. Oprah spotted Aretha Franklin, the famous singer, stepping out of the limo. Oprah hatched a quick plan. She boldly ran

*Still loved by listeners, best-selling vocalist Aretha Franklin is known as "Lady Soul."*

up to Aretha and told her a wild story—that her parents had kicked her out of the house and she needed to buy a bus ticket to go stay with relatives in Ohio. Reportedly, Aretha felt sorry for Oprah and handed her a crisp one-hundred-dollar bill. Oprah happily took the money and put herself up in a hotel for a few days. In the hotel room, she lived it up, watching TV and ordering room service.

Oprah's mother didn't understand what had happened to the sweet, quiet girl she had known just a few years earlier. She could see that something was wrong, but she didn't know what to do to help. Eventually her patience wore thin, and she looked for another home for Oprah. She called a detention home for troubled teens. But the institution was filled. Vernita decided to send Oprah back to her father's house in Nashville.

Oprah didn't know if her father would want her either, especially if he discovered the secret she was hiding. But she was heading to Nashville anyway.

*Teenage Oprah in Nashville, Tennessee*

*Chapter* **FOUR**

# PRIZE WINNER

**O**PRAH'S FATHER AND STEPMOTHER WERE HAPPY to be reunited with her. They had missed her, and they welcomed her back into their cozy house in Nashville.

But Vernon and Zelma didn't approve of Oprah's grown-up new look—her short miniskirts and heavy makeup—or her sassy new attitude. Vernon felt that Oprah's mother hadn't provided her with proper care and guidance. He was eager to get Oprah "back on track" in Nashville. When she first arrived, Oprah called her father "Pops." Vernon quickly put a stop to that. If she wanted to live in his house, he told her, she would have to follow his rules. She was to call him "Father" or "Dad," not "Pops."

Even with the rules, Oprah was glad to be back in her father's home. Compared to her mother's small apartment, Vernon and Zelma's house seemed like a mansion. They weren't wealthy, but they had plenty of food and enough money to buy clothes for Oprah. Vernon now owned his own barbershop.

At the time, Vernon had no idea that Oprah had been sexually abused in Milwaukee. Oprah hid another secret from him, too—she was pregnant. Afraid and ashamed to tell him the truth, she hid her pregnancy, wearing baggy clothing until her seventh month. At that point, Oprah's belly was noticeably round, and she knew she had to tell her father. On the day she broke the news, she was even more upset than her father was—so stressed, in fact, that she went into early labor and gave birth to the baby that day. The premature infant died within two weeks.

After her baby died, Oprah felt a mixture of sadness and relief. At age fourteen, she didn't feel ready to take on the responsibility of parenthood. Oprah never identified the baby's father.

## A Fresh Start

In September 1968, Oprah began tenth grade at East High School in Nashville. When the school year started, she was still feeling the emotional effects of losing her baby and moving to a new school. At first, her grades were almost all Cs. Vernon pushed Oprah to try harder.

"If you were a child who could only get C's, then that is all I would expect of you," he told her. "But you are not. So, in this house, C's are not acceptable."

Oprah tried to see the loss of her baby as a lesson. In a way, she had been given a second chance in life. She was determined to turn her grades, and her life, around.

Throughout high school, Oprah read avidly. She especially liked books about women who showed courage in overcoming obstacles. She read about Anne Frank, a Jewish girl who kept a diary during the years her family hid from the Nazis. She read about Helen Keller, who lived a full, rich life despite being sightless and deaf. Oprah also admired Sojourner Truth, who fought for the end of slavery and advocated women's rights long before the women's suffrage (right to vote) movement of the early 1900s.

When Oprah was sixteen, she read a book that affected her deeply, Maya Angelou's 1970 bestseller, *I Know Why the Caged Bird Sings.* Like Oprah, the main character in Angelou's autobiographical story was raised in the South by her grandmother, later lived with her mother and then her father, was raped as a child, and found comfort in books. "I read it over and over," said Oprah. "I had never before read a book that validated my own existence."

Vernon and Zelma Winfrey continued to encourage Oprah's studies as well as her public speaking. "We knew she had great potential. We knew she had a gift and talent to act and speak," said Oprah's father.

## MAYA ANGELOU

aya Angelou was born Marguerite Annie Johnson on April 4, 1928, in Saint Louis, Missouri. Her older brother, Bailey, called her "Mine" or "My," and the nickname evolved into "Maya." Shortly after her birth, Maya's family moved to San Francisco, California. When she was three, her parents divorced. Four years later, Maya was raped by her mother's boyfriend. Because of the traumatic experience, Maya refused to speak for five years.

At age sixteen, Maya became the first female streetcar conductor in San Franciso. By the time she had graduated from high school in 1945, she had given birth to a son, Clyde, whom she nicknamed Guy. Maya worked as a cook and waitress, and at age twenty-two, she married Tosh Angelos. Less than three years later, she left him and moved to New York to study dance.

During the 1950s and 1960s, Maya worked as a dancer and actor. In 1970 she published an autobiographical novel, *I Know Why the Caged Bird Sings*, under the name Maya Angelou, a modified version of Angelos.

In 1971 her first book of poetry, *Just Give Me a Cool Drink of Water 'Fore I Diiie*, was published and was nominated for a Pulitzer Prize. By 1986 Maya had published four more autobiographical novels, including *Singin' and Swingin' and Gettin' Merry Like Christmas* (1976) and *All God's Children Need Traveling Shoes* (1986).

Angelou's writing for stage, film, and television, her many novels and books of poetry, and her acting have won her countless honors and awards. She teaches at Wake Forest University in Winston-Salem, North Carolina.

"She's never been a backseat person, in school or in church. She always loved the limelight," he said.

Oprah sometimes gave Bible readings at Faith Missionary Baptist Church, which she attended each Sunday with her father and stepmother. She also spoke at other local churches and clubs.

Her talent earned her wider recognition in 1970, when she won a speech contest sponsored by the Elks Club. Oprah was nearly overwhelmed with happiness when she took the prize, a four-year college scholarship. She would begin looking at her college options next year, when she was a senior.

## THE GRAND OL' OPRAH

Besides earning good grades in school, Oprah was also popular. In 1971, her senior year of high school, she threw a big bash for her seventeenth birthday. She "borrowed" the school gym and invited everyone in the school.

That year, Oprah also ran for vice president of the student council. Her slogan was "Vote for the Grand Ol' Oprah"—a funny takeoff on the Grand Ol' Oprey, the famous Nashville auditorium that showcases country music. Oprah was thrilled when she won the election.

Later that year, Oprah and another student were selected, because of their excellent grades and leadership abilities, to represent the state of Tennessee at the White House Conference on Youth. At the conference, held in Estes Park, Colorado, Oprah met teens from all over the country. When she returned to Nashville, Oprah was interviewed by disc jockey John Heidelberg on WVOL, a local radio station. He talked to her about her experiences at the conference.

A few months later, Heidelberg called Oprah again. He asked her if she'd like to represent the radio station in the Miss Fire Prevention contest, a teen beauty pageant in Nashville. Oprah wasn't sure at first. A beauty pageant? She had never thought of herself as a "beauty," but she figured it would be fun to enter anyway.

At the pageant, Oprah paraded before the judges in her new evening gown. She didn't think she stood a chance of winning the title of Miss Fire Prevention, since no black person had ever won. And all of Oprah's opponents were white girls with "fire"-red hair. Because she didn't think she had a chance of taking the crown, Oprah felt relaxed and confident.

One part of the contest was a question-and-answer category. The judges asked each contestant a question, and the teen was supposed to come up with a thoughtful, intelligent answer. The first question was, "What would you do if you had a million dollars?"

One contestant said she would buy a truck for her father. Another teen proudly replied that she would buy her brother a motorcycle and her mother a new Frigidaire refrigerator.

Soon it was Oprah's turn to answer the question. She thought a moment. She decided just to have fun with her answer. "If I had a million dollars," Oprah began,

"I would be a spendin' fool. I'm not quite sure what I would spend it on, but I would spend, spend, spend. Spendin' fool."

The judges loved Oprah's humorous and truthful answer. They asked the contestants a second question: "What do you want to do with your life?"

The other teens all said they wanted to be teachers or nurses. Oprah hadn't really decided what she wanted to be, but she figured she had to say something unique. That morning she had seen journalist Barbara Walters on TV's *Today Show*.

"I want to be a broadcast journalist because I believe in the truth," Oprah answered. "I'm interested in proclaiming the truth to the world."

*Barbara Walters was the first news anchorwoman on a major U.S. television network.*

The judges were impressed with Oprah. She had a winning personality, and with her intelligence, she outshined the other contestants. Oprah was crowned Nashville's Miss Fire Prevention of 1971.

"I know it's not a biggie. But for me it was special," Oprah said. "I was the only black—the first black—to win the darned thing."

The sponsors at radio station WVOL were proud of Oprah. They gave her a watch and a digital clock. Even better, they asked her if she wanted to hear how her voice sounded on tape. Oprah eagerly agreed.

*Oprah's senior year high school picture, 1971*

All of her speaking experience helped Oprah sound almost like a professional news anchor. "They couldn't believe how well I read," Oprah said later. "They said, 'Come hear this girl read,' and before I knew it, there were four guys standing there listening to me read."

Even though Oprah was only seventeen years old and still in high school, she was offered a part-time job as a news reader. Oprah was thrilled. After school she hurried to the radio station to do newscasts at 3:30 P.M. She was doing something she liked, and she was getting paid for it!

## COLLEGE BOUND

In June 1971, Oprah graduated from East High School. A few months later, she entered Tennessee State University, an all-black school in Nashville, using her Elks Club scholarship. She planned to major in speech and drama. To save money, she would continue to live with her father and stepmother and commute the short distance to school. Oprah didn't want to give up her news reader job, so she continued to work part time at WVOL.

When Oprah entered college, the United States was immersed in the Vietnam War, a conflict between Communist North Vietnamese forces and U.S.-backed South Vietnamese soldiers. College students all over the country were staging angry protests against the United States' involvement in the war. In 1970 U.S. National Guardsmen had gunned down four Kent

State University students in Ohio during an antiwar protest.

Other issues also ignited students' passions. At Oprah's all-black university, many African American students were rallying for "Black Power," the empowerment of black Americans through political, and sometimes violent, activism.

"It was a weird time," Oprah said later. "This whole 'black power' movement was going on then, but I just never had any of those angry black feelings. Truth is, I've never felt prevented from doing anything because I was either black or a woman."

Oprah wasn't interested in politics or protesting. She was much more interested in succeeding in school, building on her talents, and moving ahead with her life. Because she chose not to get involved in protests during this highly political time, Oprah wasn't liked or supported by her classmates. Some students even called her an "Oreo," an expression for a black person who is considered "white on the inside and black on the outside." Oprah grew to hate college.

Shortly after starting at Tennessee State University, Oprah met and quickly fell in love with a man named William Taylor. Unfortunately, Taylor wanted to date other women, but he didn't bother to tell Oprah. When the relationship ended, Oprah was brokenhearted.

In 1972 Oprah entered and won her second beauty pageant, the Miss Black Nashville contest. She went on to win a third pageant, landing the title of Miss Black

Tennessee. Oprah was surprised to win these contests. She didn't see herself as conventionally beautiful, and she downplayed her poise, personality, and talent.

"I did not expect to win, nor did anybody else expect me to win," she said. "And Lord, were [the other contestants] upset. I said, 'Beats me, girls, I'm as shocked as you are.'"

While on a visit to Hollywood, Oprah saw the Walk of Fame on Hollywood Boulevard, where hundreds of golden stars, each matched with the name of a famous film or TV star, decorated the sidewalk. Oprah got down on her knees and rubbed one of the stars. One day, she told her father, her star would sit beside the others.

Even though Oprah's father didn't want her to be an actor, he didn't laugh. He, too, knew in his heart that his daughter was going places.

*Oprah landed her first television job while still in college.*

*Chapter* **FIVE**

# PEOPLE ARE TALKING

**I**N COLLEGE **O**PRAH ATTENDED CLASSES, STUDIED HARD, and did a lot of reading. But in her job as a news reader at radio station WVOL, she gained valuable, real-life experience.

In 1973 Oprah received a phone call from a station manager at WTVF-TV, the CBS television station in Nashville. The manager told Oprah that he had heard her on the radio and was very impressed with her talent. He wanted to hire her as a reporter for the evening news.

Oprah couldn't believe it. They wanted to hire her—as a reporter? She was only nineteen years old. Oprah didn't think she could handle both a full-time job and college. She declined the offer.

The station manager didn't give up easily. He called
Oprah two more times and tried to talk her into audi-
tioning for the job. She felt confused. She thought she
might rather be an actress than a newscaster. Oprah
asked one of her favorite speech professors at Tennessee State for advice.

"I've seen some *stupid* people," he said with a laugh.
He couldn't believe that Oprah was hesitating to accept the job. "Don't you know that's *why* people go to
college? So that CBS can call them?"

Oprah carefully considered her teacher's words. She decided to try out for the job. It could be a great opportunity.

At the audition, Oprah wasn't sure how to act. She
pretended to be TV journalist Barbara Walters. "I
would sit like Barbara, or like I imagined Barbara to
sit, and I'd look down at the script and up to the camera because I thought that's what you do, how you
act. You try to have as much eye contact as you can—
at least it seemed that way from what I had seen
Barbara do."

Oprah landed the job. She was excited about her
salary—$15,000 a year, a lot of money to her at the
time, as much as her father was making as a barber.
Best of all, she didn't have to quit school. She could
go to classes during the day and work in the evening.

At the time Oprah was hired, companies in the United
States had to comply with the new "affirmative action"
guidelines set up by the government. Businesses had to
ensure that a certain percentage of the employees they

hired were members of minority groups. Some critics accused Oprah of being a "token" at the station, a designated black person. Oprah didn't care if she was the station's token black or not. She was happy with her new job and she knew she was good at it. Not only was she the first black female newscaster in Nashville history, she was also the youngest.

## LEARNING THE ROPES

Oprah's first year as a TV news anchor had its ups and downs. One evening during a live newscast, Oprah made her first big "on-the-air" mistake.

"I was doing a list of foreign countries. . . . And I called Canada 'ca-NAD-a,'" recalled Oprah. "I got so tickled. 'That wasn't ca-NAD-a. That was CAN-ada.' And then I started laughing. Well, it became the first real moment I ever had. And the news director later said to me, 'If you do that, then you should just keep going, you shouldn't correct yourself and let people know.' So that was, for me, the beginning of realizing, 'Oh, you can laugh at yourself, and you can make a mistake, and it's not the end of the world.' You don't have to be perfect—the biggest lesson for me for television."

Oprah didn't have to be perfect, but she did want to do her best. To improve her news delivery, she studied tapes of her previous news broadcasts. She worked on her timing, rhythm, and ease in front of the camera. Soon she had developed her own warm, casual style, and she didn't copy Barbara Walters anymore.

After gaining experience at WTVF-TV, Oprah knew she wanted to continue her career in television broadcasting. She began to look around for a better broadcasting job. She sent promotional tapes of herself to stations in big cities like New York and Los Angeles.

In 1976 Oprah received a tempting job offer. The station managers at WJZ-TV in Baltimore, Maryland, offered her a job as a news reporter and anchor. They wanted her to start soon, in three months.

Oprah took some time to think it over. If she left Nashville, she'd be leaving her father and stepmother's home. She would also have to drop out of college just a few months short of earning her bachelor's degree.

But Oprah was used to fast, dramatic changes in her life. And she was determined to move forward with her career. The new job would be an upward move—a pay increase and a position at a prestigious ABC station. Oprah decided to accept the job.

## HELLO, BALTIMORE

Twenty-two-year-old Oprah arrived in Baltimore in June 1976. To advertise her upcoming debut at WJZ-TV, the station placed humorous billboards all around the city. The billboards read: "WHAT'S AN OPRAH?"

Oprah could hardly believe it. She already had a name for herself in Baltimore! She couldn't wait to start her new WJZ-TV job. Meanwhile, she rented her first apartment and shopped for new work clothes. On August 16, 1976, Oprah debuted on the six o'clock news at WJZ-TV. For the show, she wore a bright red suit. Her hair was styled in a "natural," or Afro, a popular hairstyle at the time.

Unlike most young people who are starting a new job, Oprah was calm and confident. Her years of public speaking and her anchoring experience made her comfortable in front of the cameras.

Oprah read the news in a warm and friendly style. She came across as a real, down-to-earth person. But to some people, she was a little too real for the evening news. Sometimes she changed the words that she read on the video teleprompter, to make the news stories sound more casual. And she typically became emotionally involved in the stories she reported.

"My openness is the reason I did not do so well as a news reporter," Oprah said. "I used to go on assignment and be so open that I would say to people at fires—and they'd lost their children—'That's okay. You don't have to talk to me.'"

Oprah's news director wasn't as understanding. He said, "What do you mean they didn't have to talk to you?" Oprah replied, "But she just lost her child, and you know I just felt so bad."

For one assignment, Oprah was sent to report on a funeral, and she refused to go into the funeral home. She felt compassion for the families involved, and she didn't want to disturb anyone. Sometimes when Oprah was reading an especially sad story, she would even cry on the air.

Oprah's bosses didn't appreciate her natural and open style of reporting the news. In Nashville, audiences had liked her easygoing, friendly manner. But the people of Baltimore expected a more polished news anchor. Oprah didn't have the slick, conservative appearance of the other news anchors in town.

## CLOUDS AND SILVER LININGS

Oprah had signed a two-year contract with the station, so the managers couldn't fire her. Instead, they took her off the evening news and gave her a five-minute time slot at 5:30 in the morning. She had been moved, the bosses said, because she was "so good" that she needed her own time slot. But Oprah knew better. She had been demoted.

"I was devastated because up until that point, I had sort of cruised," she said. "I really hadn't thought a lot about my life, or the direction it was taking. I just happened into television, happened into radio. . . . I was twenty-two and embarrassed by the whole thing because I had never failed before."

Meanwhile, the station managers decided that Oprah needed a makeover, a change in her appearance. They sent her to an expensive salon in New York to have her hair straightened and styled. Oprah wondered about their reasons for the decision. Did her bosses want her to look more like the white newscasters?

The results of the salon session were disastrous. The hair stylist left the harsh straightening chemicals on for too long, damaging Oprah's hair so badly that it fell out. For weeks she had to wear a wig.

Things didn't get better. The executives at WJZ-TV didn't like Oprah's speaking voice, either. They arranged for her to take lessons from a professional voice coach at a local broadcasting school. Oprah became depressed. Her job didn't feel right at all. But she figured she had no choice but to change the way she talked and looked if she wanted to keep her job.

Reluctantly she dragged herself to the voice coach's office. But, to her surprise, the coach didn't think there was anything wrong with her voice. All Oprah needed to do, the teacher said, was to learn to speak up for herself. She shouldn't let anyone try to change her into someone she wasn't. The coach warned that Oprah would never make it in broadcasting if she didn't stand up to her bosses.

But Oprah wasn't even sure she wanted to make it in broadcasting. In her heart, she still dreamed of being an actress.

"I really don't want to do this. What I want to do is act," Oprah told the voice coach. "What I think is going to happen is that I will be discovered because I want it so badly. Somebody is going to have to discover me."

"You are a dreamer," said the coach.

Oprah didn't care if she was a dreamer. She headed back to WJZ-TV with a new attitude. She would just ride this out—take the morning news spot and bide her time until something better came along.

While Oprah's professional life in Baltimore was

rocky, in her personal life she made a new friend, Gayle King, another WJZ-TV newscaster. One evening a sudden snowstorm left Gayle stranded at the station. Oprah invited her to stay over at her apartment, near the studio. The two bonded instantly, delighting in the discovery that they wore the same dress and shoe sizes and even had the same contact lens prescription. They soon became best friends.

Oprah's work life began to improve in 1978, when a new station manager was hired at WJZ-TV. He wanted Oprah to cohost a new morning talk show called *People Are Talking*. Oprah and her cohost, Richard Sher, would be interviewing famous and lesser known celebrities. The show would feature lighthearted, fun interviews as well as serious, personal stories.

*Oprah found a lifelong friend in Gayle King. This is a promotional picture for the show* Just Between Friends *that they later hosted together.*

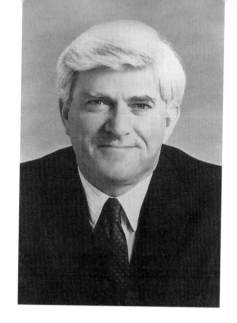

Phil Donahue helped create the daytime talk show format and was Oprah's friendly competition.

The new show was a perfect fit for Oprah. "The day I did that talk show, I felt like I'd come home," she said. She recalled, "My very first interview was the Carvel Ice Cream Man, and Benny from *All My Children*—I'll never forget it. I came off the air, thinking, 'This is what I should have been doing.' Because it was . . . like breathing to me. Like breathing."

On *People Are Talking,* Oprah could be herself— warm, friendly, and funny—and viewers liked it. She loved talking with her guests about issues and feelings. And she instantly clicked with her cohost, Richard Sher, who had previous experience as a talk show host.

At first the management at WJZ-TV was nervous about the new show. *People Are Talking* would air during the same time slot as *The Phil Donahue Show,* a very popular, nationally syndicated talk show.

But within weeks, the executives relaxed. *People Are Talking* had a larger Baltimore audience than Donahue's show. Women viewers, especially, loved Oprah.

*Sofia, a character in* The Color Purple, *is a strong-willed woman who doesn't back down in the face of abuse and racism. Oprah played Sofia,* above, *in the film version of the novel.*

# Chapter **SIX**

# *THE OPRAH WINFREY SHOW*

**T**WENTY-EIGHT-YEAR-OLD **O**PRAH **W**INFREY **FLIPPED** through the pages of the *New York Times Book Review,* just as she did every Sunday morning. She always read the book review section of the newspaper from cover to cover.

An article about a new book by African American author Alice Walker caught her eye. The book, *The Color Purple,* was about a "poor, barely literate Southern black woman who struggles to escape the brutality... of her treatment by men," the review said.

The novel sounded very interesting to Oprah. She read the whole book in one day. Then she bought every copy of *The Color Purple* in stock—she wanted to share it with friends.

Celie, the main character in the story, has survived great hardship and abuse. She writes letters to God, talking about her roles in life and the powerful black women who shape her life.

Oprah could relate to Celie on a deep level. "I read the first page of *The Color Purple,* put the book down, and wept," Oprah said. "I could not believe it, that someone had put this in writing. It was unbelievable."

The book was very healing for her, she said, because "you know that you are not the only one. Because all of this time, you have carried this burden. You think nobody else in the world has been through this. Nobody else is as *bad* as you. And then you discover that you are not so bad after all. It's an amazing thing." Oprah liked *The Color Purple* so much that she gave copies of the book to the staff and crew of *People Are Talking.*

## FATEFUL AUDITION

Oprah cohosted the top-rated Baltimore talk show for six years. In the fall of 1984, when she was thirty, another big opportunity came her way. A colleague at WJZ-TV told her about a job opening at WLS-TV in Chicago, hosting a talk show called *A.M. Chicago.* If Oprah landed the job, she would get a huge salary increase, close to $200,000 a year.

On Labor Day, Oprah flew to Chicago and recorded a one-hour audition tape, speaking informally about herself and a variety of topics. The station manager,

# ALICE WALKER

lice Malsenior Walker was born in Eatonton, Georgia, on February 9, 1944. Alice, her parents, and her seven older siblings lived in a small, crowded shack that they rented from a white farmer. When Alice was eight years old, one of her older brothers accidentally shot her in the eye with a BB gun, leaving her blind in one eye. Fortunately, the impairment didn't dampen Alice's interest in reading and learning. She was valedictorian of her high school class and won a scholarship to Spelman College in Atlanta, Georgia. Two years later, she transferred to Sarah Lawrence College in New York and earned her bachelor of arts degree in 1965.

Shortly after she graduated from college, Alice moved to Tougaloo, Mississippi, and became active in the Civil Rights movement. She married a lawyer, Melvyn Leventhal, in 1967, and they had a daughter, Rebecca. They divorced in 1976, and soon afterward, Alice moved to San Francisco, where she wrote poetry, short stories, essays, and fiction. Her early works include the novels *The Third Life of Grange Copeland* (1970) and *Meridian* (1976) and the poetry collections *Once* (1968) and *Revolutionary Petunias & Other Poems* (1973). In 1982 Walker published *The Color Purple,* which won the Pulitzer Prize. The book has been published in twenty-two languages and has sold over four million copies.

In the years to follow, Walker wrote many more books, including *In Search of Our Mothers' Gardens: Womanist Prose* (1983), *Living by the Word* (1988), *The Temple of My Familiar* (1989), *Possessing the Secret of Joy* (1992), *By the Light of My Father's Smile* (1998), and *The Way Forward Is with a Broken Heart* (2000). She has earned countless awards, including the Lillian Smith Award from the National Endowment for the Arts.

Dennis Swanson, reviewed her audition tape in his office.

"I'm looking at this and I'm thinking to myself, 'Oh my goodness, I'm not this lucky,'" remembered Swanson. "This is the greatest audition tape I have ever seen."

Later that day, Oprah met with Swanson in his office. He wanted to hire her, but he didn't "let on" immediately.

"*What* do you think?" asked Oprah.

"I think it went pretty well," answered Swanson.

Oprah worried that her skin color might hurt her chances of getting the job. "You know I'm black," she said.

"I'm looking at you," replied Swanson matter-of-factly.

"And you know I have these kind of weight issues," Oprah said. "I've been trying to lose weight."

"And so have I," said Swanson, smiling. "Nobody around here is going to complain about that!"

Swanson walked over to Oprah and pretended to measure her head on her shoulders.

"What are you doing?" she asked.

"Your head fits very nicely on your shoulders," said Swanson. "I just want to make sure that when this great success befalls you that it [your head] will always stay there."

"Do you really think I could be that successful?" said Oprah, realizing that she had landed the job.

"Yes, I do," Swanson replied. He added that the station would be in contact with her soon to draw up a contract for her new position at *A.M. Chicago.*

## TOP-RATED TALKER

Chicago, Illinois, the "Windy City" on Lake Michigan, is one of the biggest cities in the country. It was also the home base for Phil Donahue, Oprah's talk show rival. Could she keep up the top ratings she had scored in Baltimore?

Phil Donahue had pioneered the format that Oprah used in her talk show, in which the host, holding a microphone, goes into the audience and allows people to make comments or ask questions of the show's guests. Donahue had a straightforward style and focused on issues in an impersonal way, much like a news reporter.

Oprah, on the other hand, "got personal" on her show. She shared her own feelings, insecurities, and secrets with her viewers. On a show about weight loss, for example, Oprah revealed her own struggle with food addiction. Once, she said, she devoured a whole package of hot dog buns as a midnight snack, first defrosting them in the microwave and then smothering them with maple syrup.

Oprah connected with her guests and her audience. When a guest was upset, Oprah usually gave her a hug or touched her hand. She was a different kind of talk show host.

"The closest thing that Phil Donahue ever talked about was the fact that he was a wayward Catholic," commented another talk show host, Maury Povich. "Other than that, talk show hosts didn't talk about themselves. Oprah opened up a lot of new windows because [viewers] could empathize with her."

Because Oprah shared her feelings, guests were inspired to talk openly about their problems, too. "My ability to get people to open up is [because] there is a common bond in the human spirit," Oprah said. "We all want the same things. And I know that."

Oprah loved her job. She didn't think things could get any better—but they did. A year after she moved to Chicago, in 1985, her show got a new name: *The Oprah Winfrey Show*. And the program soon topped *The Phil Donahue Show* in the Nielsen ratings, a measure of how many viewers watch a particular television show. Despite her show's success, Oprah felt like something was missing in her life. She had always wanted to act in a film, not just be a TV host.

## THE COLOR PURPLE

One day in 1985, film producer and musician Quincy Jones was in Chicago on business. He turned on the TV and spotted Oprah hosting her hit talk show. He knew immediately that she was right for the part of Sofia in the film he was currently producing, *The Color Purple*—the movie version of the book that Oprah loved so much.

Jones didn't waste time. Oprah was soon given the chance to audition. A few months later, Steven Spiel-

*Quincy Jones and Oprah on the set of* The Color Purple

berg, the film's director, called Oprah and offered her the role. Oprah had been "discovered," just as she had dreamed of for so long. She called it "absolutely divine intervention." In the film, Oprah played Sofia, a woman who fights back against an abusive husband named Harpo, played by Danny Glover. Released in December 1985, *The Color Purple* received mixed reviews. Oprah's performance, however, was praised. *Newsweek* magazine called her portrayal of Sofia "a brazen delight."

In 1986 Oprah was nominated for an Academy Award for her performance in the film. She arrived at the Oscars dressed in a glamorous, bead-trimmed, gold and ivory gown. She also wore a diamond necklace and earrings and a ten-thousand-dollar fox fur coat,

Oprah in Los Angeles, California, in 1986. Her popularity was growing but so was her struggle with her weight.

dyed bright purple in a play on the movie's title. Oprah looked stunning, but she felt fat. Her dress was so tight she could hardly breathe during the ceremony.

Throughout her career, Oprah had often turned to food for comfort when she felt stressed or overwhelmed. As a result, she had steadily put on weight, and at the 1986 Academy Awards ceremony, she was almost at her heaviest point.

When she didn't win an Oscar, Oprah tried to make light of her disappointment as well as her weight problems. "Perhaps God was saying to me, 'Oprah, you are not winning because your dress is too tight for you to make it up all those steps to receive the statuette,'" she told a writer for *McCall's* magazine.

Oprah tried not to be too discouraged about her loss at the Academy Awards. She knew that just being nominated for an Oscar was a great honor in itself. She also knew that she wanted to continue acting in films.

Meanwhile, *The Oprah Winfrey Show* continued to receive top ratings. In 1986 Oprah signed a deal with King World Productions, Inc., a TV syndication company. This meant that the show was broadcast nationally. People across the country got to know Oprah, the first African American host of a national TV talk show.

Oprah's fame soon grew to celebrity proportions. In the late 1980s, she was driving to a speaking engagement with her best friend, Gayle. As they pulled closer to the auditorium where Oprah was to speak, the two friends could see police cars, long lines, and a big crowd of people. A traffic jam clogged the street.

"Who's coming?" asked Gayle.

"I am," said Oprah.

"No, no, I mean, who is really coming? Besides you? Who are all of these policemen for?"

"Me," said Oprah, laughing.

Gayle was shocked. "Oh, my goodness," she said. "What is becoming of you?"

## HARPO PRODUCTIONS

Another benefit of national syndication was that Oprah made a lot more money—nearly $125 million a year. With her increased income, Oprah decided to form her own production company, Harpo (Oprah spelled backward) Productions, Inc. With the creation of Harpo, Oprah became one of the first women in history to own a TV and film production company, following in the footsteps of pioneering studio owners Mary Pickford, an actress in silent films, and Lucille Ball, the comedian and actress. Oprah broke other ground, too.

Through her new company, Oprah began to buy the film rights to literary works, such as Toni Morrison's 1987 novel, *Beloved*. By purchasing the rights to literary works, Harpo reserved the right to make movies based on those works. Harpo could produce a film version of a book many years after the rights were acquired. The company purchased the rights to several novels, including *Their Eyes Were Watching God* by Zora Neale Hurston and *The Wedding* by Dorothy West.

Besides getting Harpo off the ground, Oprah continued to devote herself to her talk show. Whether the program was about child abuse or divorce or being overweight, she strove to let people know that they had the power to change their lives.

Oprah also stressed the importance of dealing with the past and healing emotional pain. "If you don't heal your personal wounds, they continue to bleed," she said. "And so we have a country of people who have continued to bleed."

In the early 1990s, *The Oprah Winfrey Show* began to change, focusing more on personal development and spiritual growth. Oprah hosted guests such as inspirational speaker Marianne Williamson, who encouraged people to reach for their best selves.

Oprah agreed with Williamson's philosophy. "As a kid . . . I always wanted to be a minister and preach and be a missionary," said Oprah. "And I think, in many ways, that I have been able to fulfill all of that. I feel that my show is a ministry."

But Oprah isn't just a speaker. "She does something that most people don't have a clue about—she knows how to listen," commented musician and producer Quincy Jones. "And she listens not just with her head. She listens with her heart and soul."

In 1987 Oprah accepted her first Daytime Emmy Award, for Outstanding Talk Show Host. Her show also won Emmys for Outstanding Talk Show and Outstanding Talk Show Director.

## LOVE IN THE AIR

While Oprah's TV and film career was going very well, her personal life lacked romance. That changed in 1987, when she met a man who would stay by her side for years to come.

Stedman Graham was a good-looking, six-and-a-half-foot-tall former model and basketball player. He worked as the executive director of a nonprofit program called Athletes Against Drugs. He had been married once and had a young daughter, Wendy. Oprah had met Stedman at fund-raisers and parties around Chicago, but she had never spent time with him.

One day Stedman called Oprah and asked her for a date. Oprah thought he seemed nice, and she was very

Stedman Graham, right, is originally from Whitesboro, New Jersey. He played professional basketball in Europe before returning to the United States and entering the business world.

attracted to him. But she was afraid that Stedman liked her just because she was famous and wealthy, so she turned him down. Stedman was determined, however. He called Oprah several times, each time asking her for a date. Finally she gave in and went out with him. Within weeks, their casual dates turned into a serious, committed relationship.

Oprah reached another professional milestone in 1988, when Harpo Productions bought the rights to *The Oprah Winfrey Show*. Now Oprah could produce her own show her own way. She planned to change the format from a live broadcast to pretaped shows, giving her more flexibility and free time in her schedule. She also wanted to find a new studio for the show and a more attractive, comfortable working environment for her staff.

She was thinking big. She spent $10 million on an 88,000-square-foot production studio, one-half mile west of downtown Chicago. She then laid down another $10 million to remodel the block-long facility, adding a TV studio, staff gym, posh offices, and a screening room complete with a popcorn machine. She named the new studio Harpo Studios.

Oprah's empire continued to grow. A few months later, in 1989, she opened a restaurant with Chicago restaurateur Richard Melman. The unusual restaurant, called the Eccentric, featured the food and decor of four different countries—the United States, England, France, and Italy. The American menu offerings included some of Oprah's favorite dishes, including "Oprah's potatoes," made with potatoes, horseradish, parsley, and cream.

The greater Oprah's power and fame became, the more the press seemed to harass her. Although Oprah

*Located on Erie Street in downtown Chicago, the Eccentric was one of the city's hot spots.*

and Stedman were very happy together, media people hounded them about their relationship. "Why aren't you married?" reporters repeatedly asked. The media, especially tabloid newspapers such as *The National Enquirer*, wrote mean-spirited stories suggesting that Stedman only stayed with Oprah for her money.

Sometimes the press made rude comments about Oprah's weight. She was deeply upset by the articles. "The tabloids used to make me cry all the time," she said. "Every time they would come out with the least little thing about me, I used to [cry]."

## WEIGHTY ISSUES

The stories were all the more painful because Oprah desperately wanted to lose weight. In 1988, during the summer break from her show, she went on a severe liquid diet. For three and a half months, she restricted herself to a commercial diet drink. Because the diet was so extreme, a doctor monitored her progress. Oprah also started working out at a gym and jogging. By the time the fall television season began, she had lost sixty-seven pounds.

On November 15, 1988, Oprah shared her weight-loss victory with her viewers. She appeared onstage dressed in tight-fitting, size ten designer jeans. She pulled a wagon filled with sixty-seven pounds of animal fat, symbolizing her weight loss. The audience clapped and cheered Oprah's success.

Other viewers were not so approving of her newly

*Oprah after losing sixty-seven pounds*

thin figure. For many people, Oprah Winfrey had been admirable because she could be fabulously successful without being thin. What message was she sending now about body image? Some viewers felt that Oprah had let them down.

But Oprah wasn't happy being overweight. She wanted to lose weight for herself more than anyone else. She felt healthy and more confident. However, as is common for people who follow rapid weight-loss programs, Oprah gained the weight back quickly.

Oprah's ups and downs on the scale did not slow her career success. Her show continued to pick up top ratings and several awards. Nonetheless, the tabloid press continued to taunt her. About three years after Oprah and Stedman got together, rumors circulated that Stedman was gay.

"That was the most difficult time for me," said Oprah. "I believe in my heart that had I not been an overweight woman, that rumor would never have occurred. If I were lean and pretty, nobody would ever say that. What people were really saying is why would a straight, good-looking guy be with her?"

"He was so brave," Oprah added. "And I never loved him more. He taught me so much during that period. When I handed [the article] to him, he looked at it and said, 'This is not my life. I don't have anything to do with this.'"

Oprah was learning the huge challenges of being a celebrity. She couldn't walk alone with Stedman at a park, for example, without photographers following them. In 1989 Oprah bought a 160-acre farm in Indiana—a retreat from the world and her celebrity status. The property included an eight-room guest house, a charming log cabin, a gym, a pool, and a barn with nine horses.

"I've never loved a place the way I love my farm," Oprah told a writer for *Essence* magazine. "I grew up in the country, which is probably why I'm so attached to the land. . . . I love the lay of the land. I love walking the land. And I love knowing that it's my land."

Oprah liked spending time on her farm because she could unwind there and be herself. She didn't have to be "on"—smiling for the cameras. Underneath her stardom, she was a regular person, with problems like anyone else. In 1989 she grieved the loss of her brother Jeffrey, who died of AIDS. Although Oprah had not been in close contact with Jeffrey, his death still hit her hard.

Oprah hasn't talked much publicly about her family members or her relationship with them. Of all her relatives, Oprah credits her grandmother, Hattie Mae Lee, for shaping her life the most. "My grandmother gave me the foundation for success that I was allowed to continue to build upon," Oprah said. "My grandmother taught me to read, and that opened the door to all kinds of possibilities for me."

*Oprah claims another Daytime Emmy Award for Outstanding Talk Show Host in 1991.*

*Chapter* **SEVEN**

# NEW
# DIRECTIONS

**I**N **1990 O**PRAH **BROADCAST AN EPISODE OF HER** talk show that changed the way she looked at herself. She was interviewing a woman with multiple personalities who had been severely abused as a child. In the middle of the show, listening to the woman's story, Oprah recalls, "[I thought] 'Oh, that's why I was that way.' I always blamed myself. Even though, intellectually, I would say to other kids, I would speak to people and say, 'Oh, the child's never to blame. You're never responsible for the molestation in your life.' I still believed I was responsible somehow. That I was a bad girl.

"So it happened on the air, as so many things happen for me. It happened on the air in the middle of someone else's experience, and I thought I was going to have a breakdown on television. And I said, 'Stop! Stop! You've got to stop rolling cameras!' And they didn't, so I got myself through it, but it was really quite traumatic for me.

"And I realize that I was the kind of child who was always searching for love and affection and attention, and somebody to . . . look at me and say, 'Yes, you are worthy.' Unfortunately, there are adults who will take advantage of that and misread your intentions."

The show was a turning point for Oprah. From then on, she tried to overcome her need to be a "people pleaser." She worked on changing her old pattern of wanting everyone to like her. She was determined to overcome the effects of her childhood abuse.

"It's a wonder she's not off in a corner drooling," joked Oprah's friend Gayle. "She has not only made it—she has flourished."

Oprah realized that she could use her painful past in a positive way, to help other victims of abuse. "A part of my mission in life now is to encourage every other child who has been abused to tell. You tell, and if they don't believe you, you keep telling," Oprah said. "You tell everybody until somebody listens to you."

In 1991 Oprah told the nation's lawmakers about her abuse. She testified before the U.S. Senate Judiciary Committee and worked for the passage of the National Child Protection Act, which established a nationwide database of convicted child abusers.

A couple of years later, President Bill Clinton signed "Oprah's Bill" into law.

## TAKING CONTROL

In June 1992, Oprah accepted her third Daytime Emmy Award for Outstanding Talk Show Host. But, instead of being happy, she was humiliated, she said, at having to "waddle my way up to the stage with the nation watching my huge behind." Oprah's weight had climbed to an all-time high of 237 pounds.

*In 1992 Oprah received her third Daytime Emmy Award for Outstanding Talk Show Host.*

"I felt like such a loser, like I'd lost control of my life," she remembered. "I was the fattest woman in the room."

For Oprah, eating was triggered by uncomfortable feelings, such as anxiety, sadness, and fear. "Just some indication that there might be some stress next Thursday would cause me to start eating right now," she said. "If the plumbing guy was coming over and I was afraid he was going to be upset if I complained about the bill. If I was afraid I was going to have to tell somebody something that would make him the slightest bit uncomfortable, my coping mechanism was food. I'd think: 'I gotta eat. I gotta eat. I gotta eat.' Then I'd feel calmer."

After the Emmy Awards, Oprah went to a spa in Telluride, Colorado, to lose weight. There she met personal trainer Bob Greene. Oprah liked Greene immediately. He was warm and friendly, and he didn't have a TV, so he didn't know anything about her. Oprah asked Greene to develop a fitness program for her.

Oprah lost more than ten pounds at the spa, by following a low-fat diet and Greene's exercise program. She felt better than she had in years. Her personal life was going well, too. In 1992 Stedman proposed marriage to Oprah, and the couple set a wedding date for the following September.

Oprah had another announcement to make—she was writing her autobiography. She was busy and happy, and she was looking good, too. Oprah talked Bob Greene into moving to Chicago to be her personal trainer.

Greene accepted the offer, but he insisted that Oprah begin her fitness program gradually. At first, she walked each day. She worked her way up to jogging three miles a day, then eight miles a day. She worked out six days a week, and when she went on vacation, Greene went with her. He was as dedicated to Oprah's fitness as she was. A few months later, Oprah completed a thirteen-mile half-marathon in San Diego.

The emphasis of her new fitness program was good health, not just losing weight. She also got support from her personal chef, Rosie Daley. Daley kept Oprah on a diet of delicious, low-fat food. By 1993 Oprah had shed almost ninety pounds.

She felt like she was finally getting to the bottom of her weight issues. "You need to understand what's really eating you," she said. "For me it was my inability to face the truth about my life in every aspect. I learned very early to deny my feelings about my own pain. . . . And so you build layers on top of that and bury it. I just covered everything up."

In June 1993, Oprah announced that she wouldn't be writing her autobiography after all. It wasn't the right time to tell her story, she said.

"That's probably the toughest thing for Oprah to do, is to commit to something and not follow through," commented Bob Greene. "It was really tough [for her]."

Oprah did not follow through on her wedding plans, either—the September wedding date came and went. But Oprah and Stedman remained a couple.

## HELPING OTHERS

While Oprah did not write her autobiography, she released a different kind of book for her fans in 1994. She and her chef, Rosie Daley, published *In the Kitchen with Rosie*, a cookbook of low-fat recipes by Daley. The day after Oprah promoted the book on her show, it sold at a record-breaking rate, and it remained a best-seller for almost a year.

Although Oprah was very wealthy and famous, she found joy in helping others to achieve success. After a 1993 appearance on Oprah's show, Deepak Chopra, an Indian-born doctor, saw his book *Ageless Body, Timeless Mind* shoot to the top of the best-seller lists.

In 1994 Oprah found a unique way to help people. She hosted a charity event at Chicago's Hyatt Regency Hotel, an auction of her previously worn designer clothing and shoes.

One woman who went to the auction was a poor, single mother. She could only afford a five-dollar pair of shoes, size ten. She wouldn't be able to wear the shoes, because her feet were size seven, but she wanted the shoes anyway. The woman later met Oprah after a taping of her show. She told Oprah, "Sometimes I go in the closet when I'm feeling down and I stand in your shoes."

"That story makes me want to weep," said Oprah. "It makes me think I must be doing something right."

Although the ratings for *The Oprah Winfrey Show* were high, Oprah continued to look for ways to improve the quality and content of her program. She was tired of broadcasting shows about dysfunctional families, feuding relatives, and messed-up lives.

"I was in the middle of a show with some white supremacist, skinheads, Ku Klux Klan members," Oprah remembered, "and I just had a flash, I thought, 'This is doing nobody any good—nobody.' I had [told myself], 'Oh, people need to know that these kinds of people are out here.' I won't do it anymore."

Oprah preferred to uplift and inspire viewers. In May 1995, she launched a six-week series on her show called "Get Movin' with Oprah." With the series, she hoped to motivate viewers to embrace fitness and exercise.

## OPRAH'S BOOK CLUB®

She also wanted to share her love of books with her viewers. "What a difference it makes in your world to go into some other life. It's what I love most. I'm reading always to leave myself, always to leave myself behind," said Oprah. "That's what reading is. You get to leave."

In 1996 Oprah established an on-the-air reading group, Oprah's Book Club®. On her show, she assigned a book for viewers to read. One month later, book club members would tune in for a discussion with the author of the book.

Oprah's first book club selection was *The Deep End of the Ocean,* a novel about a family coping with the disappearance of a child. The book's author, Jacquelyn Mitchard, saw a similarity among many of the books—and authors—chosen for the book club. "All of the authors that she has picked for the book club were lonely children whose refuge was in books," Mitchard remarked. "Oprah is clearly in that club."

The book club selections were unusual, intense, serious stories, such as *Rapture of Canaan* by Sheri Reynolds, about a fourteen-year-old girl who joins a cult and becomes pregnant, and *She's Come Undone* by Wally Lamb, a novel about a young, overweight victim of abuse.

Oprah's Book Club® was an immediate hit. The show's audience members were inspired to go out and buy the books that Oprah recommended. The club got more people reading, and the literary community became more interested in the show. Book sales soared, creating a new surge in the book publishing industry. The popularity of book groups increased, too. People across the country formed their own book groups.

Book publishers were not prepared at first for the tremendous demand generated by Oprah's show. According to Philip Pfeffer, chief executive officer of the Borders bookstore chain, the "Oprah phenomenon" was the biggest change to hit the publishing industry in fifteen years.

*Toni Morrison was the first African American woman to receive the Nobel Prize for fiction.*

"Oprah Winfrey has been able to generate interest in reading through her book club," Pfeffer said. "The thing that's amazing to me is *Oprah Winfrey* airs at 4 P.M. The show is not watched by what we consider our core customer base. But Oprah's viewers go out and buy the books featured on the show."

Oprah also invited established, well-known writers such as Toni Morrison, the author of award-winning books like *Song of Solomon* and *Beloved,* to be part of the book club. Oprah called Morrison "the greatest living American writer, male or female, white or black."

In 1996 Oprah featured a book on her talk show that

*Oprah and her trainer, Bob Greene,* left, *coauthored* Make the Connection: Ten Steps to a Better Body—and a Better Life.

she herself had a part in creating. In *Make the Connection: Ten Steps to a Better Body—and a Better Life*, Oprah discusses her struggles with weight loss. She and personal trainer Bob Greene outline a day-by-day fitness plan, using a positive, self-loving approach.

"I love this book because for so many years I struggled and wanted to be Diana Ross," Oprah told the crowd at a book promotion at Soldier Field in Chicago. "Then I realized no matter what I did I was not gonna have Diana's thighs! I realized that I just have to settle into what is the best body for me."

Oprah was learning to love herself more—and to feel joy in her life. "I used to say I didn't have time to experience joy. I had too much to do," she said. "But I started to be aware of the life I'm living. . . . Now when we're running, I smell the jasmine; I notice when there's a pack of butterflies."

*Many famous national figures, such as senator and former first lady Hillary Rodham Clinton,* above, *have appeared on Oprah's popular talk show over the years.*

*Chapter* **EIGHT**

# A WOMAN WITH WINGS

**I**N **1997** OPRAH LAUNCHED A CHARITY CAMPAIGN called Oprah's Angel Network®. The goal was simply to make the world a better place to live. Each year for three years, the network gave college scholarships to fifty young people chosen by the Boys and Girls Clubs of America. Each recipient received a $25,000 college scholarship. Oprah also encouraged viewers to create their own "mini-miracle" by donating their spare change to the scholarships and adding to the "world's largest piggy bank."

Oprah and the Angel Network® also planned to build more than two hundred "Oprah Houses" for Habitat for Humanity, an organization that helps needy families build decent, affordable housing. By the summer of

1998, Oprah's Angel Network® had collected more than $3.5 million from corporate sponsors.

Oprah's efforts continued on all fronts in 1997. That year Harpo launched production of "Oprah Winfrey Presents"—a series of six high-quality made-for-television movies on ABC.

The first of these movies, *Before Women Had Wings,* debuted in November 1997. The film, based on the novel by Connie May Fowler and starring Oprah Winfrey and Ellen Barkin, was about a poor, abused girl named Bird Johnson. A few months later, in February 1998, *The Wedding* aired. Other films in the ABC series included *Amy and Isabelle,* the story of a mother and daughter's struggle to overcome haunting secrets, *David and Lisa,* a love story about two emotionally disturbed teens, and *Tuesdays with Morrie,* the true story of a man's weekly visits with his dying former teacher.

Also in 1997, Oprah released a videotape version of the book *Make the Connection.* She told a *Chicago Tribune* newspaper reporter that the video, *Oprah: Make the Connection,* was "about how to take control of your life. I am now about trying to convince people to stop wasting time. I know it's hard because it's much easier to want to believe there's some kind of magic fix coming along."

On April 30, 1997, Oprah made a guest appearance on *Ellen,* a hit sitcom starring the comedian Ellen DeGeneres. On the show, Oprah played the role of

Ellen's therapist, counseling her about "coming out of the closet" as a gay person. In one scene, Oprah said to Ellen, "Good for you, you're gay!"

Oprah's appearance on the show stirred up controversy. Rumors that Oprah herself was gay soon circulated in gossip columns across the country. People wondered why she and her boyfriend, Stedman, had never gotten married as they had planned.

On June 4, Oprah told the press, "Lotta rumors circulatin' that I'm gonna be coming out. I am not in the closet. I am not coming out of the closet. I am not gay." Oprah told reporters that she had simply wanted to support her friend Ellen in the groundbreaking episode.

Stedman talked to the press about the incident, too. "She's not [gay]. Oprah knows who she is," he told *People* magazine. Even though he and Oprah had postponed their marriage indefinitely, their bond as a couple remained strong.

Oprah was always looking for ways to make her talk show livelier and more interesting. In mid-1997, she told her TV audience that she would be taping an upcoming Oprah's Book Club® show at the home of poet and novelist Maya Angelou. Angelou, whom Oprah has called "the woman who has had, undoubtedly, the greatest influence on my life," had written the nonfiction book *The Heart of a Woman*.

However, Oprah had forgotten to "OK" the book club party beforehand. When Oprah made the announcement, Maya, watching the show at home, started laughing. She shouted at the television, "But you haven't spoken to me!"

Oprah won her over, and in June 1997, Maya threw an on-the-air book club pajama party at her home in Winston-Salem, North Carolina. Maya, Oprah, and four other women, all wearing comfy pajamas, discussed *The Heart of a Woman*. Afterward, Maya served a big, home-cooked meal.

## TROUBLE IN TEXAS

Oprah's commitment to informative, high-quality television eventually got her in trouble. On April 16, 1996, an episode of *The Oprah Winfrey Show* entitled "Dangerous Food" had aired. On the show, Oprah's guests talked about the risks of bovine spongiform encephalopathy, or "mad cow disease," which allegedly could cause a related disease in humans who ate beef from affected cattle.

At one point in the show, a vegetarian activist talked about the dangers of the frightening disease, which has never occurred in the United States. Oprah blurted out, "It has just stopped me cold from eating another burger."

Oprah's comment made some people furious, especially a group of Texas cattle ranchers. The cattlemen filed a lawsuit against Oprah, claiming that she had "wrongfully defamed" American beef and cost the cattle industry millions of dollars.

In January 1998, Oprah, then forty-four, traveled to Amarillo, Texas, for the trial. She brought her staff from Harpo Productions with her. Oprah appeared in court every day for the trial, then taped her talk show after leaving the courthouse.

Joe Coyne, the chief attorney for the cattle ranchers, was rough on Oprah and her talk show. "They ran out of psychics talking to the dead and put on this show instead," he said.

In public Oprah remained composed and calm throughout the trial. But in her private life, she was afraid. While most of the citizens of Amarillo were friendly and welcoming, Oprah worried that a "random fanatic excited by all the controversy" might hurt her. Anxious and overwhelmed by the situation, Oprah gained eleven pounds during the course of the trial.

After six weeks, the Texas jury found that Oprah was not liable for damage to the beef industry because of her controversial statements during the 1996 "mad cow" program. All the charges that had been brought against her were dismissed.

"Free speech not only lives, it rocks!" Oprah happily announced at the end of the trial. "I will continue to use my voice," she said. "I believed from the beginning that this was an attempt to muzzle that voice. And I come from a people who have struggled and died in order to have a voice in this country, and I refuse to be muzzled."

A joyful Oprah won the lawsuit brought against her by cattlemen in Amarillo, Texas.

## BELOVED

While she has not been an activist for African American rights, Oprah has always felt a strong sense of pride in her heritage. In 1997 she began production on a new project that was particularly meaningful to her. Ten years earlier, she had read Toni Morrison's novel *Beloved*. Oprah was so moved by the book that she called Morrison the next day. Oprah told the author that Harpo Productions wanted to buy the film rights to the book.

At first Morrison was amused by Oprah's offer. She didn't think that a film could be made of her book, but she agreed to the deal.

"It was truly an honor to write that check as one black woman to another," said Oprah. "No agents. No lawyer. No negotiations. Just 'This is what you asked for and here it is.'"

In the film, directed by Jonathan Demme, Oprah played Sethe, an escaped slave living on a farm in Ohio in 1873. Sethe is haunted by her memories of the Sweet Home plantation—and by the ghost of her baby daughter. Sethe is reunited with another ex-slave who escaped from Sweet Home, Paul D, played by Danny Glover.

Oprah knew that making the film wasn't going to be easy. But she didn't know just how hard it would be, on an emotional level, to play the role of Sethe and to really grasp the impact of slavery.

"I thought I knew it," she said. "But what I have come to know is that I had just intellectually understood it—the difficulty, the sorrow, the pain. You can talk about it on an intellectual level, but during the process of doing *Beloved,* for the first time, I went to the knowing place."

To prepare for her film role and get a closer sense of what it was like to be a slave, Oprah took part in a historical "reenactment" of slave times. She was

*Oprah played Sethe in* Beloved *along with Danny Glover, right, who played Paul D.*

dumped, barefoot and alone, in the Maryland woods, at a spot that used to be part of the Underground Railroad, where runaway slaves once traveled. White men acting the part of slave traders harassed her and called her names. Oprah felt strong and unafraid at first, but then she broke down.

"I became hysterical. It was raw, raw, raw pain," said Oprah. "I went to the darkest place, and I saw the light. And I thought, 'So this is where I come from.'"

On the movie set, Oprah honored the lives of African American slaves by keeping ownership papers in her trailer as a reminder of the brutal reality of slavery. These documents listed slaves by name and prices, such as Big John, $900, Sarah, $800, and Little Anna, $200.

"I would have all of those documents laid out, and every morning I would light candles and say a prayer for each of them," Oprah recalled. "I would call their names out loud. And then I would go in and do the scene. I'd say, 'I'm doing this for you, Little Anna.' Or, 'Today is Big John's Day.' And when I had trouble on the set, I would go into a corner and call them up."

After the filming of one emotional scene, Oprah could see that her costar, Danny Glover, was very upset. Oprah put her arms around him and asked him what was wrong.

Glover told Oprah that he had "seen" some of the characters in the book while doing the scene. "I felt myself drowning," he said. "I saw Sixo [a slave] being burned. I saw [all the slaves at Sweet

Home]. . . . Oprah, I felt them; I felt their breath."

Oprah held Glover for a long time as he wept. "I just held on to her," remembered Glover, "until I felt like I could come back."

The experience of making *Beloved* stayed with Oprah long after filming was over. "The first time I saw [the film], I thought they were going to have to carry me out," she said. "Every single image caused such intense, deeply felt emotions."

"*[Beloved]* was the dearest thing to Oprah's heart," observed Gayle King. "She felt more passionate about it than anything I've seen her do."

*Beloved* was first released in movie theaters in October 1998. Movie critic Roger Ebert called Oprah's acting "a brave, deep performance." Peter Travers of *Rolling Stone* magazine wrote, "Winfrey's pitch-perfect performance as Sethe, besides being the stuff for which Oscars are molded, resonates with beauty, terror and the kind of truth that invades dreams.

"[Critics] who resent her TV success . . . her wealth, her book clubs, her influence over popular culture will just have to shut up and eat crow. She's that good."

While the film received good reviews, it did not fare well at the box office. On the weekend *Beloved* opened, a movie called *Bride of Chuckie* was the top movie.

"*Bride of Chuckie?*" remembered Oprah's friend Gayle. "We thought we were at least going to the Oscars, and instead nobody liked the movie."

Oprah was disappointed by the public's response to the film. But she had grown as a person by making the movie. She had also formed a solid bond with the book's author, Toni Morrison. Oprah invited her friend to her farm in Indiana.

Morrison appreciated Oprah's book-filled home. "Except for other writers' [homes], I have very seldom seen a home with so many books—all kinds of books, handled and read books," said Morrison. "She's a genuine reader, not a decorative one. She's a carnivorous reader."

Besides reading, Oprah enjoyed spending time with friends and with Stedman. "I decided that I wanted to have more fun in my life, and I've been having a ball," she said in 1998.

*Oprah,* left, *and Rosie O'Donnell,* right, *show off their awards at the 1998 Daytime Emmy Awards at Radio City Music Hall in New York City.*

*Chapter* **NINE**

# SKY'S THE LIMIT

**S**INCE *THE* **OPRAH** **WINFREY** *SHOW* **BEGAN,** **THE**
show and Oprah had been winning Daytime Emmy
Awards practically every year. In 1998 the National
Academy of Television Arts and Sciences presented
Oprah with a Daytime Emmy Award for Lifetime
Achievement. She also tied with Rosie O'Donnell for
the Outstanding Talk Show Host award.

O'Donnell is one of Oprah's biggest fans. "Oprah set the
standard in daytime television," O'Donnell said. "She con-
sistently maintains a decency and morality on her show
that gives talk shows a positive name."

In the fall of 1998, Oprah began a new season of her
show with what she called "Change Your Life TV." On
one program in the new format, the guest was John

Gray, author of the best-selling self-help book *Men Are from Mars, Women Are from Venus*. Gray, who stresses that men and women handle emotions differently, encouraged couples to work out their problems in constructive, creative ways. Oprah also added a new segment to the show called "Remembering Your Spirit," which showed how viewers, who are mostly women, could take time for themselves and nurture their spiritual lives.

With twenty-six million viewers nationally tuning in each week, *The Oprah Winfrey Show* remains the highest-rated talk show in history. An estimated twenty-five thousand letters and e-mails arrive at Harpo Productions each week. *The Oprah Winfrey Show* is seen in 112 countries, including South Africa, China, and Israel. Oprah is the wealthiest female entertainer in the world, with an estimated fortune of $725 million.

## STAYING CENTERED

Being a celebrity isn't always easy. How does Oprah handle the pressures of fame and success? She starts each day with quiet meditation. Every morning, she prays, "Dear God, my heart is open to you. Come sit in my heart." Oprah explains, "I say that to myself over and over and try to think of what I can do to make somebody feel really good today."

Oprah's routine also includes daily exercise. In the city, she uses a treadmill and a StairMaster. At her farm in Indiana, she likes to hike or jog in the fields.

On her days off, Oprah likes to stay at her farm and read, relax, and play with her dogs. Seven of the dogs live permanently on the farm in Indiana, while her two cocker spaniels, Sophie and Solomon, whom she calls "small humans with fur," are her constant companions.

Almost every day, Oprah chats on the phone with her best friend, Gayle, who launched her own short-lived talk show in 1997. "I never feel far from Oprah, no matter where she is," says Gayle, who worked as a newscaster in Connecticut. "I know that I can always count on her, and that's a very powerful thing. And she knows the same is true for me."

Oprah says of Gayle, "In spite of all the things that have happened to me, we laugh every night about one thing or another. She absolutely keeps me grounded."

Oprah often treats her loved ones to fun getaways and parties. And Stedman is still a big part of Oprah's life. He continues to be "a pillar of support in my life, not only in our relationship, but also as a trusted advisor," she says.

In June 1999 and again in 2000, Oprah and Stedman taught a business course together at Northwestern University's Kellogg Graduate School of Management. The course, "Dynamics of Leadership," was held one night a week for ten weeks. "It has always been a dream of mine to teach," said Oprah. "When Stedman invited me to be a part of his class, I jumped at the opportunity."

The media continues to question Oprah about her relationship with Stedman. The couple has remained "engaged" for years. "I think we have deep love and caring for each other and respect," Oprah says. "Every day we get asked a question. . . . 'When are you getting married?' And I say it works so well the way it is, I wouldn't want to mess it up."

In 2000 cable television's Arts and Entertainment (A&E) Network aired a biography of Oprah. The program drew a record-breaking 4.8 million viewers.

## MEDIA SUPERWOMAN

In 1998 Oprah announced plans to invest in Oxygen Media, a venture that includes Geraldine Laybourne and Carsey-Werner-Mandabach. Oxygen Media includes a women's cable network, which launched in

*Oprah gets a hug from her longtime boyfriend, Stedman.*

February 2000. Harpo's "Online with Oprah" at <www.oprah.com> is linked to the Oxygen channel. Oprah's online resource is available to millions of users every day.

"It's an extension of who I am and what I want to be in the world," says Oprah of the Oxygen Network. "[We've] created a wonderful platform to bring women to themselves as best we know how. There's not better work. Sometimes we get giddy."

*Newsweek* calls Oprah Winfrey "one of the most powerful brand names in the entertainment industry." This means that anything with the name Oprah on it is bound to be a success.

In May 2000, Oprah teamed up with Hearst Magazines to launch yet another new venture—her own magazine. *O: The Oprah Magazine* features encouraging articles and inspirational stories. The first issue of *O* hit newsstands in mid-2000. It sold out its premiere issue which, after an additional print run of 500,000, totalled 1.6 million copies.

Oprah demanded perfection from the *O* staff. "Look," she told the staff. "I know that to you guys the Oprah name is a brand. But for me, it's my life . . . and the way I behave and everything I stand for."

Each month, Oprah writes a column for the magazine. In the debut issue, she wrote about her mission for the magazine: "How far can you grow? What will it take for you to fulfill your potential? My hope is that this magazine will help you lead a more productive

life, one in which you feel a sense of vitality, coopera-
tion, harmony, balance and reverence for yourself and
in all your encounters."

Some critics say that Oprah acts too much like a
preacher or a psychologist on her show and in the
magazine. "She's turned a bit too preachy for me
these last few years," commented one *Oprah* viewer on
an online message board. "I still watch for certain
guests now and then, but Oprah herself kinda turned
me off with her armchair shrink act."

But millions of people continue to seek inspiration
from Oprah. In June 2000, Oprah brought her
"Personal Growth Summit," a self-help seminar,
to auditoriums in four cities. "I'm not here
to preach to anyone about how to run your life," she
told the crowd at the first summit, in Detroit. "I just
know what worked for me and I'm here to
share it."

"Oprah is a good mentor for us black women," said
seminar attendee Janet Graham, a thirty-six-year-old
counselor for abused women and children. "She's been
through a lot and nothing's been handed to her. . . . It's
inspiring. How big do you dream, especially if
you've never seen anyone who looks like you reach
that high? Because of her, other women reach
higher."

Oprah continues to give not only her time to people,
but her money as well. She is the national spokes-
woman for A Better Chance. In July 2000, she wrote a

check for $10 million to the organization, which places gifted minority students in top schools across the country.

Despite her tremendous career success, Oprah still struggles with very human issues, such as her weight. "I eat when I'm happy, I eat when I'm sad, I eat when I'm depressed," Oprah says. "I eat when I can't decide am I happy, depressed or sad. I say, 'Let me have some potato chips and decide.'"

Her wealth doesn't make Oprah immune to problems. "I am so rich I cannot believe it," Oprah said at a Personal Growth Summit meeting. But, she added, "Every issue y'all have had, I've had it too. That's what money does, it magnifies everything."

Oprah opened her 2000–2001 season premiere show, on September 11, with a special guest, then vice president and presidential candidate Al Gore. A week later, Gore's opponent, Texas governor George W. Bush, received equal time on the show.

At one point in Oprah's television interview with Vice President Gore, she asked him how he got all his energy for his exhausting campaign. Gore answered, "If you believe in what you are doing, then you get more energy."

Gore pointed out that Oprah had found renewed energy when she changed the direction of her show. "And you told your audience, 'Hey, take a chance with me—let's do this differently,'" said Gore. "When you started believing in what you were doing, [it gave you

*George W. Bush appeared on Oprah's talk show in September 2000 during the presidential campaign.*

energy]...now look at you—you're a one-person media conglomerate!"

Oprah remains humble in spite of her fame. She doesn't see herself as a leader or a preacher or a teacher anymore. At heart, she doesn't think she's different from anyone else.

"I'm just a voice trying to help people rediscover their best selves," she says. "All of us have that within us. [It's like] *The Wizard of Oz,* when Glinda, the Good Witch, tells Dorothy, 'You've always had it, my dear.' You've always had the power. Everyone has the power inside."

# SOURCES

7   "Oprah Winfrey: Entertainment Executive," *Academy of Achievement* interview, February 21, 1991, <http://www.achievement.org> (August 23, 2000).

9   Ron Stodghill, "Daring to Go There," *Time*, October 5, 1998, 80.

10   "Oprah Winfrey: Entertainment Executive."

10   Ibid.

11   Marilyn Johnson, "Oprah Winfrey," *Life*, September 1997, 44.

12   Norman King, *Everybody Loves Oprah* (New York: William Morrow and Co., 1987), 34.

12   Audreen Buffalo, *Meet Oprah Winfrey* (New York: Random House, 1993), 27-28.

13   "Martin Luther King, Jr.," *Encyclopedia Britannica 2000*, n.d., <http://www.britannica.com> (October 23, 2000).

15   Johnson, 44.

16   Jenny Allen, "Oprah Winfrey," *US Weekly*, June 12, 2000, 67.

18   Johnson, 44.

18   "Oprah Winfrey: Entertainment Executive."

19   Ibid.

19   "The Creation," The Academy of American Poets, n.d., <http://www.poets/org/poems> (October 22, 2000).

22   "That's the Wonderful Thing about Great Teachers: Every One Is an Inspiration to Somebody," CTA Quest, n.d., <http://www.ctaquest.org/quest_quest/1_oprah/oprah.html> (September 1, 2000).

23   John Culhane, "Oprah Winfrey: How Truth Changed Her Life," *Reader's Digest*, February 1989, 102.

24   "Oprah Winfrey: Entertainment Executive."

24   *Oprah Winfrey: Heart of the Matter*, prod. Eileen Lucas, 120 minutes, ABC News Productions for A&E Networks, © 1999 ABC Inc. and A&E Networks, videocassette.

24   Joan Barthel, "Oprah!", *Ms.*, August 1986, 56.

25   Johnson, 44.

26   "Oprah Winfrey: Entertainment Executive."

26–27   King, 48.

27   Ibid; Ibid., 49.

28   Ibid.

33   Culhane, 103.
33   Johnson, 44.
33, 35   King, 62.
36   "Oprah Winfrey: Entertainment Executive."
36–37   Ibid.
37   Ibid.; Ibid.
38   King, 63.
39   "Oprah Winfrey: Entertainment Executive."
40   King, 75.
41   Audrey Edwards, "Oprah Winfrey, Stealing the Show," *Essence*, October 1986, 52.
44   King, 78; Ibid., 79.
45   "Oprah Winfrey: Entertainment Executive."
47   Ibid.
48   Ibid.
49   Ibid.
51   Allen, 67.
51   "Oprah Winfrey: Entertainment Executive."
53   Johnson, 44.
54   "Oprah Winfrey: Entertainment Executive."
54   Ibid.
56   *Oprah Winfrey: Heart of the Matter.*
57–58   "Oprah Winfrey," Mr. Showbiz, n.d., <http://www.mrshowbiz.com> (June 23, 2000).
58   "Oprah Winfrey: Entertainment Executive."
59   Johnson, 44.
59   David Ansen, "We Shall Overcome," *Newsweek*, December 30, 1985, 60.
60   Leslie Rubenstein, "Oprah! Thriving on Faith," *McCall's*, December 1987, 140.
61   "Girlfriends Are Forever," *Good Housekeeping*, May 2000, 110.
62   "Oprah Winfrey: Entertainment Executive."
63   *Oprah Winfrey: Heart of the Matter.*
66   Laura B. Randolph, "Oprah Opens Up about Her Weight, Her Wedding and Why She Withheld the Book," *Ebony*, October 1993, 130.
68   Ibid.
68   Pearl Cleage, "Walking in the Light," *Essence*, June 1991, 48.
69   "Oprah Winfrey: Entertainment Executive."
71–72   Ibid.

72   Lisa Russell and Cindy Dampier, "Oprah Winfrey,"
     *People Weekly,* March 15, 1999, 143.
72   "Oprah Winfrey: Entertainment Executive."
73   Joanna Powell, "I Was Trying to Fill Something Deeper,"
     *Good Housekeeping,* October 1996, 80.
74   Ibid.; Ibid.
75   Ibid.
75   *Oprah Winfrey: Heart of the Matter.*
76–77   Russell and Dampier, 143.
77   "Oprah Winfrey: Entertainment Executive."
77   Johnson, 44.
78   Ibid.
79   Arthur Bridgeforth Jr., "Internet, *Oprah,* Enliven Sluggish
     Book Industry," *Crain's Detroit Business,* January 18, 1999, 27.
80   Johnson, 44.
81   Powell, 80; Ibid.
84   "Oprah Winfrey Gives Her Weight Loss Tips in New Video,
     'Oprah: Make the Connection,'" *Jet,* October 20, 1997, 23.
85   Kristen Baldwin and Albert Kim, "Grapevine Formula,"
     *Entertainment Weekly,* June 20, 1997, 9.
85   "Nope, She's Not Gay," *People Weekly,* June 23, 1997, 66.
85   Ibid.
85   Johnson, 44.
86   Ibid.
86   Laurel Brubaker Colkins and Craig Tomashoff, "Oprah
     1, Beef 0," *People Weekly,* March 16, 1998, 59.
87   Ibid.
88   "Oprah Says She Felt Redeemed after Victory over Texas
     Cattlemen," *Jet,* March 23, 1998, 22.
89   Greg Spring, "Thrilla in Amarilla," *Electronic Media,*
     March 2, 1998, 2.
89   Ibid.
89   Oprah Winfrey and Pearl Cleage, "The Courage to
     Dream!", *Essence,* December 1998, 80.
91   Laura B. Randolph, "Oprah and Danny," *Ebony,*
     November 1998, 36.
91   Stodghill, 80.
92   Randolph, 36.
92   Ibid.
92   Ibid.

92  Ibid.
92  "Oprah Winfrey," *People Weekly,* December 28, 1998, 86.
92  Ibid.
92–93  Peter Travers, "Oprah . . . Oscar; Oscar. . . Oprah," *Rolling Stone,* October 29, 1998, 79.
93  "Girlfriends Are Forever," 110.
93  Johnson, 44.
93  Leslie Marshall and Dana Fineman, "The Intentional Oprah," *InStyle,* November 1998, 338.
95  Larry Mayer et al., *The Soul and Spirit of a Superstar, An Unofficial Tribute: Oprah Winfrey* (Chicago: Triumph Entertainment, 2000), 14.
96  Joanna Powell, "Oprah's Awakening," *Good Housekeeping,* December 1998, 112.
97  "Girlfriends Are Forever," 110.
97  "Gayle King Makes Talk Show History with Oprah and Stedman," *Jet,* October 20, 1997, 54.
97  "Stedman Graham," © 1997 The Seattle Times Co., <http://www.speakers.com/sgraham.html> (August 14, 2000).
97  "Oprah Winfrey and Beau Stedman Graham to Teach Class at Northwestern University," *Jet,* June 7, 1999, 20.
98  "Gayle King Makes Talk Show History With Oprah and Stedman," 54.
99  Lynette Clemetson, "The Birth of a Network," *Newsweek,* November 15, 1999, 60.
99  Ibid.; Allen, 67.
99–100  Oprah Winfrey, *O: The Oprah Magazine,* September 2000, n.p.
100  AZZIZZ, *Deja.com,* n.d., <alt.support.diet.low-carb> (October 28, 2000).
100  Mimi Avins, "Flocking to the Church of Oprah," *Los Angeles Times,* June 25, 2000. Access through EBSCOhost®, EBSCO Information Services Group, article no. 000059965445082000.
100  Ibid.
101  Allen, 67.
101  Avins.
101–102  *The Oprah Winfrey Show,* September 11, 2000, HARPO Entertainment Group, Chicago, IL.
102–103  Powell, 112.

# SELECTED BIBLIOGRAPHY

## BOOKS

Greene, Bob, and Oprah Winfrey. *Make the Connection: Ten Steps to a Better Body—and a Better Life.* New York: Hyperion, 1999.
King, Norman. *Everybody Loves Oprah.* New York: William Morrow and Co., 1987.

## NEWSPAPER AND MAGAZINE ARTICLES

Allen, Jenny. "Oprah Winfrey." *US Weekly,* June 12, 2000.
Clemetson, Lynette. "The Birth of a Network." *Newsweek,* November 15, 1999.
Culhane, John. "Oprah Winfrey: How Truth Changed Her Life." *Reader's Digest,* February 1989.
Farley, Christopher John. "Queen of All Media." *Time,* October 5, 1998.
"Girlfriends Are Forever." *Good Housekeeping,* May 2000.
Grossberger, Lewis. "The Story of O." *MediaWeek,* April 24, 2000.
Johnson, Marilyn. "Oprah Winfrey." *Life,* September 1997.
Malcom, Shawna. "Oprah Mania." *Entertainment Weekly,* September 4, 1998.
"Oprah Winfrey." *Biography,* December 1998.
Powell, Joanna. "Oprah's Awakening." *Good Housekeeping,* December 1998.
Randolph, Laura B. "Oprah Opens Up about Her Weight, Her Wedding and Why She Withheld the Book." *Ebony,* October 1993.
Russell, Lisa, and Cindy Dampier. "Oprah Winfrey." *People Weekly,* March 15, 1999.
Winfrey, Oprah, and Pearl Cleage. "The Courage to Dream!" *Essence,* December 1998.

## VIDEOS

*Oprah Winfrey: Heart of the Matter.* Produced by Eileen Lucas. 120 min. ABC News Productions for A&E Networks. © 1999 ABC Inc. and A&E Networks. Videocassette.

# INDEX

*Oprah with a fan*

# OTHER TITLES FROM LERNER AND A&E®:

Arthur Ashe
The Beatles
Benjamin Franklin
Bill Gates
Bruce Lee
Carl Sagan
Chief Crazy Horse
Christopher Reeve
Edgar Allan Poe
Eleanor Roosevelt
George W. Bush
George Lucas
Gloria Estefan
Jack London
Jacques Cousteau
Jane Austen
Jesse Owens
Jesse Ventura
Jimi Hendrix
John Glenn
Latin Sensations

Legends of Dracula
Legends of Santa Claus
Louisa May Alcott
Madeleine Albright
Malcolm X
Mark Twain
Maya Angelou
Mohandas Gandhi
Mother Teresa
Nelson Mandela
Princess Diana
Queen Cleopatra
Queen Latifah
Rosie O'Donnell
Saint Joan of Arc
Thurgood Marshall
William Shakespeare
Wilma Rudolph
Women in Space
Women of the Wild West

# ABOUT THE AUTHOR

Katherine Krohn is the author of several biographies for young readers, including *Marilyn Monroe: Norma Jeane's Dream, Elvis Presley: The King, Rosie O'Donnell, Princess Diana, Ella Fitzgerald: First Lady of Song,* and *Women of the Wild West.* She lives in the Pacific Northwest with her dog, Lucky, and her cats, Ursula and Mr. Peterman. Ms. Krohn is also a fiction writer and an artist.

## PHOTO ACKNOWLEDGMENTS